P I L G R

✠

DURHAM

Also available in the *Pilgrim Guide* series

P I L G R I M · G U I D E

DURHAM

*The Cathedral Church of Christ
and Blessed Mary the Virgin
in Durham*

Stephen Pedley

CANTERBURY
PRESS
Norwich

© G. S. Pedley 1997

First published in 1997 by The Canterbury Press Norwich
(a publishing imprint of Hymns Ancient & Modern Limited
a registered charity)
St Mary's Works, St Mary's Plain
Norwich, Norfolk NR3 3BH

British Library Cataloguing in Publication Data

A catalogue record for this book is available
from the British Library

ISBN 1-85311-171-6

Typeset, printed and bound in Great Britain by
The Lavenham Press Ltd,
Lavenham, Suffolk, CO10 9RN

Contents

The Cathedral from Palace Green

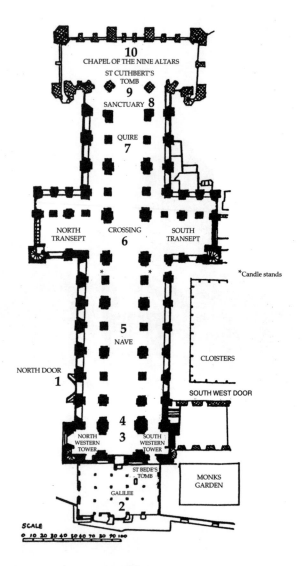

10
CHAPEL OF THE NINE ALTARS

ST CUTHBERT'S
TOMB
9

SANCTUARY **8**

QUIRE
7

NORTH
TRANSEPT

CROSSING
6

SOUTH
TRANSEPT

*Candle stands

5
NAVE

CLOISTERS

NORTH DOOR
1

SOUTH WEST DOOR

4
3

NORTH
WESTERN
TOWER

SOUTH
WESTERN
TOWER

MONKS
GARDEN

ST BEDE'S
TOMB

GALILEE
2

SCALE
0 10 20 30 40 50 60 70 80 90 100

1

Arrival through the North Door

Welcome to Durham Cathedral.

This book may seem to be written for the Christian pilgrim to Durham. Though the Christian is in mind, it is hoped that this 'reading' of the Cathedral may help anyone coming to it in a reflective, meditative way.

You have approached the Cathedral from Palace Green on the north side. Behind you is the Castle, which was once one of the houses of the Bishops of Durham. Many of these Bishops have played an important part in our national life. The Castle is now part of the University of Durham, which is the third oldest university in England. And behind you too is the market-place and the City of Durham, a place of trade, administration and commerce, with links around the world.

The Cathedral was begun in 1093 and the original Quire and Nave were finished forty years later in 1133. In 1104 the principal focus inside the Cathedral was the altar in the Quire, with the shrine of St Cuthbert behind it. The western towers and the central tower, all of which you can see well as you approach the north door, were finished later. The Cathedral was the church of the largest and most significant Benedictine monastery in the North of England. With the support of the Norman bishops, it was specially planned and built by the monks for their worship of God. This was centred on the Quire behind a stone screen. But visitors and pilgrims were always welcome in the Nave. It was always a very busy place. Most of the monks left in 1539 when the monastery was surrendered to Henry VIII. The last Prior became the first Dean. With twelve other monks, the

The Sanctuary Knocker

Cathedral carried on under the care of the Dean and Chapter. The present five residentiary canons and the Dean continue the ministry of worship and prayer for which the Cathedral was first built.

You have entered a great sanctuary – a holy space set apart for God and for those seeking him. In different times and in different ways there have always been such sanctuaries. Fixed to the north door is the replica of the famous sanctuary Knocker, a marvellous piece of twelfth-century bronze-work. Most churches in the Middle Ages had rights of sanctuary, but few of them still have visible signs of this. A criminal, arriving at the door and claiming protection, used the Knocker to get the attention of two watchmen who were in the chamber over the door. He was granted the protection of the Church and could choose between trial and voluntary exile. We do not use the Cathedral in that way today, but many people come to it from all over the world seeking help, peace of mind, quiet, the answer to a prayer, or a sense of the presence of God.

We do not know the names of the original builders or much about them. There must have been hundreds of them. We do know, however, that they did their work to the best of their ability. They knew that they were building on good foundations. Because the Cathedral is built largely on solid rock, there was no need for a crypt or any secondary foundation (unlike York Minster, which was built on a Roman camp!). The Norman builders knew that they could build on a large scale – a scale not seen in England before. In the end they were able to cover the entire building with stone vaulting instead of a wooden ceiling, making it safe from fire and giving it a sense of unity. Those who first visit Durham marvel at the high quality of the stonework. Because of the good foundations and the fine craftsmanship, the Cathedral today is largely as its builders left it.

> Come into his gates with thanksgiving
> and into his courts with praise;
> give thanks to him and bless his holy name.
>
> (Psalm 100:3)

Now that you have arrived, think of the Cathedral as a place of sanctuary and prayer, a holy space set aside for God in the middle of a busy city to remind us that God is present to us wherever we are. This place is built on a firm foundation – God himself. It has been built, cherished and used for over 900 years by those wanting to be close to him. God offers us a foundation for our lives.

> Almighty God,
> to whose glory this house of prayer is dedicated:
> we thank you for the many blessings
> you have given us
> and to those who come to worship here;
> and we pray that all who seek you in this place may
> be found by you,
> and being filled with the Holy Spirit
> may become a living temple acceptable to you;
> through Jesus Christ our Lord. Amen.[1]

The Coat of Arms of the Cathedral

2

The Galilee Chapel

Stand at the back of the Nave near the Font and pause as you look around you. Give the building time to speak to you! All that you see was completed in about forty years.

Behind the west door is the Galilee Chapel. There are entrances either side to north and south. As you enter the Galilee you will find at once a change effected by the architecture. It is lighter than the Nave. This, the first addition to the Cathedral, was built in the 1170s by Bishop Hugh de Puiset, a great patron of the arts. It is believed that Puiset, following the fashion of the day, wanted to build a Lady Chapel at the east end of the church. Poor foundations, or a disgruntled Cuthbert (whose anxieties about women even extended to the Virgin Mary), made him change his plans.

Instead he built the Galilee Chapel at the west end, close to the edge of the steep river-bank, and it was used as a Lady Chapel.

In the fifteenth century the Galilee was remodelled by Cardinal Langley, whose tomb in front of the west door is all that remains of his chantry chapel. He heightened the aisles, gave them new timber roofs, and replaced the original

The Galilee Arches

small windows with larger ones. Because of quarrying on the riverbanks below, the Galilee had become insecure. Langley built the buttresses which now support it outside. Even so, this is the one part of the Cathedral that potentially is on the move!

The large Galilee Chapel had a particular function in the weekly worship of the monastery. Processions from the High Altar ended here to remind the community that the disciples met Christ after his resurrection in Galilee. Now that the statue of the Annunciation stands at the centre of the Chapel, it reminds us today of the importance to the Church of Mary, the mother of Jesus. Without Mary there would have been no Jesus, so that God would not have been able to share our human life. The statue is contemporary and is Polish.

The Galilee windows contain an interesting collection of glass, some medieval and some modern. Not all of it is of Durham origin. In the south-west corner is the earliest representation of a wedding ceremony in English stained glass. It dates from Langley's time and is all that survives of a Seven Sacraments window. The modern windows on the north side commemorate Mary and Bede.

The tomb of the Venerable Bede is on the south side of the Galilee. Bede was born in 673 in what is now Sunderland. He spent his life based in the monastery at Jarrow where he had access to a fine library. He became a great scholar and was well-known throughout Western Europe. He wrote many works, including *A History of the English Church and People*, a life of St Cuthbert, commentaries on Scripture and sermons. He was also a mathematician and a measurer of time. He died in 735. In 1020 his bones were brought to Durham and after the completion of the Galilee, they were placed here. In the Middle Ages pilgrims came to Bede's shrine as well as to St Cuthbert's. Perhaps it was the memory of Bede the scholar

St Bede's Tomb, Galilee Chapel

that inspired Langley in the fifteenth century to found a permanent school in Durham.

In the Galilee we think about Mary and her faith in God. The Chapel, which is lighter than the Nave, reminds us of the promise and expectation of youth. This is the least secure part of the Cathedral. Our faith, like Mary's, has its fragile moments. We need the support of each other's prayers and the prayers of the Church if we are to know God's presence with us. Like Mary and Bede, we are called to reflect on God's dealings with us and to learn from them. 'Mary kept all these things in her heart' (Luke 2:19).

> We beseech you, O Lord,
> to pour your grace into our hearts;
> that as we have known the incarnation of your Son
>   Jesus Christ
> by the message of an angel,
> so by his cross and passion
> we may be brought to the glory of his resurrection;
> through Jesus Christ our Lord.[2]

If you leave the Galilee on the north side, notice close behind the altar the strikingly beautiful twelfth-century wall painting of St Cuthbert. He is portrayed as a bishop. Opposite is St Oswald, the king. These are the only sizeable remains of the Cathedral's internal wall decorations.

3

The Font and its Cover

You have moved back into the Nave of the Cathedral. At the west end of the Nave stands the Font with its splendid and unusual wooden canopy or cover.

In the Middle Ages the Font was in the Galilee because that was the place which was most accessible to the general public. Remember that the Cathedral you are standing in now was built for the particular needs of the monastic community which used it as its place of worship. The original interior would have looked different. At the head of the Nave, between the two votive candle stands, there was once a stone screen. In front of it was an altar called the Jesus Altar. On top of the screen was a carving of the Crucifixion. Mary, Jesus' mother, and St John stood on either side, with cherubim and seraphim. It would have been impossible to see beyond the screen to the Quire and to the rose window. It is difficult to imagine what the Nave would have been like. It must have been darker and much noisier than it is today.

The monastery was surrendered after 450 years to Henry VIII in 1539. It is difficult to know exactly what happened then and afterwards, or to know how people felt about all the changes. From 1539 to 1660 a lot of damage was done to the Cathedral. The windows were broken, the statues and the images of the saints were damaged, and the interior decoration was despoiled or whitewashed. At the time of Charles I an attempt was made to restore things. The Civil War stopped that. The last straw in this sad tale of despoilation came in 1650, when the Cathedral was used to house prisoners of war taken captive by Oliver Cromwell at the battle of Dunbar. They finished off what others had started. By 1660, when Charles II was restored as King of England

The Font

and the bells rang out (if there were any left), the interior of the Cathedral must have looked bleak and unloved.

Charles II appointed a new Bishop of Durham named John Cosin, who had been a member of the Chapter here earlier under Charles I, just at the time when the first attempts were being made to restore 'the beauty of holiness' to the Cathedral. When he returned in 1662 he was determined to try again where once he had failed. He rebuilt his Castle and remodelled Palace Green. He helped publish a new Prayer Book for the Church of England – *The Book of Common Prayer* which we still use. He encouraged the restoration of many churches in the diocese, and he began an extensive restoration of the Cathedral which has continued in one way or another from his day to ours.

He provided the Cathedral with a marble Font. He placed it at the west end close to the main door because he wanted to remind us that it is through the sacrament of Baptism that we are made one with Christ and so become members of Christ's Church. He emphasized the importance of Baptism by also providing the cover or canopy that stands over the Font. This cover is crowned with a dove, the symbol of the Holy Spirit – the dove that descended on Jesus at his Baptism in the River Jordan.

Bishop Cosin also linked this Font to the overall design of the Cathedral's interior layout. Taking the pinnacles of the late fourteenth-century Neville Screen behind the main altar as his 'design theme', he built new screens to the north and south of the altar, and he made new stalls for the clergy and the choir. In this way, at the east end of the Cathedral, he emphasized the sacrament of Holy Communion, through which our membership of Christ's Church is nourished and strengthened. Cosin linked together the two sacraments of the New Testament – Baptism and Holy Communion – giving the Cathedral a visual unity for the Anglican sacramental worship which continues to be the centre of devotion here.

We give thanks to God for John Cosin and for all who have worked to beautify this church, making it a place for worship, recollection and hearing the call of God. Standing by his Font, we are reminded of the importance of Baptism in the life of every Christian. Like Mary, we are called to fulfil God's promises, and our Baptism commits him to us and us to him.

✠

The Lord is my strength and my song
And has become my salvation.

Almighty God, we thank you for our fellowship in
the household faith with all those who have been
baptized in your name. Keep us faithful to our
baptism, and so make us ready for that day when
the whole creation shall be made perfect in your
Son, our Saviour Jesus Christ. Amen.[3]

4

The Black Bar in the Floor

Just to the east of the Font the pilgrim will notice a bar of black Frosterley marble laid in the pavement of the Nave floor. Although we cannot be certain about its precise origin or meaning, we do know that this bar has been in this position since the Middle Ages. It was there to mark the limit beyond which no woman could cross in the time of the monastery – for fear of St Cuthbert's wrath. When in the twelfth century Puiset's plans for a Lady Chapel at the east end of the Cathedral, and thus close to Cuthbert's shrine, foundered on poor foundations, it was believed that Cuthbert was expressing his distaste for women and for their sexuality, which potentially posed such a problem to his community of monks. This prejudice is difficult for us to understand today.

There is nothing in Bede's life of Cuthbert to suggest that he had a publicized dislike of women. As a Christian monk and bishop, evangelizing and preaching in heathen Northumbria, he would have been aware of sexual sins as part of human sinfulness in general. He was on good terms with all the early Christian leaders of Northumbria, some of whom, like St Hilda of Whitby, were women who consulted Cuthbert.

St Cuthbert's body was brought to Durham in 995. A group of secular clergy built up the religious centre that was in part designed to protect the shrine. Some of these clergy would have been married. In the late eleventh century the Normans moved Benedictine monks in to replace the secular canons as the guardians of the shrine and to reform its life. So women's access to the church gradually became much more restricted. Those who broke through the barrier in disguise in order to pray at the shrine were severely disciplined! How long these restrictions were in force we do not know. Perhaps the issue waxed and waned. Something, at any rate, was at the bottom of 'the story of the bar'. It seems an injustice to believe that Cuthbert was involved. Today, when there is a just concern for the safety and rights of women, the bar receives an attention which is quite out of proportion to its historical importance.

Whatever way we react to the bar on the floor, today it serves to remind pilgrims of the prejudice and intolerance that exists not just in institutions like the Church but also within our own hearts and minds. Legend (whatever its basis in historical fact) and the falsification of truth have a terrifying power to shape our attitudes and behaviour towards one another. For us today racial prejudice is an example of this power. Ignorance about the past can destroy us. As pilgrims, baptized into the community of Christ, we must recognize the darkness which is in and around us. We pray that through the grace of the Holy Spirit we may be willing to allow our darkness to be overcome by God's light, and we pray that we may always be forgiven as we seek the truth of God.

O Lord, open our lips;
and our mouths shall proclaim your praise.

Almighty God, you forgive all who truly repent;
have mercy upon us,
deliver us from all our sins,
confirm and strengthen us in all goodness,
and bring us to eternal life;
through Jesus Christ our Lord. Amen.[4]

14

5

The Nave

The pilgrim crosses the bar, mindful of the continuing need for repentance and forgiveness, and walks confidently into the open space of the Nave. Look up and look around!

The Nave was completed by 1133. So the vault above our heads has stood for over 850 years. The ribs of the vault are decorated with dogtooth ornament, popular with the Normans, and the big transverse arches that divide the bays are pointed. This is probably the last and the finest Romanesque vaulted Nave to be built in Western Europe. Within seven years the first purely Gothic vaults were designed and constructed in the eastern ambulatory at St Denis, north of Paris, and Western architecture would never be the same again — at least until the Victorian revivalists! So when the Nave was built, in engineering and architectural terms, this was a creative time.

The Nave pillars are remarkable for their size and strength, and especially for their deeply carved patterns. Near the altars of the Cathedral the pillars all have a spiral pattern. Here in the Nave the variety is stunning. Pillars in large churches were often patterned by colour-ing. These pillars were copied in several other churches for which the Durham monks were responsible. We assume that much of the interior surface of the Cathedral was coloured (in blues, reds, greens and gold), but we cannot be sure. The windows were all filled with glorious stained glass.

View across Nave

Imagine this tremendous space without pews and chairs. The weak sat on the wall ledges. Notice the arcaded dado running along the length of the aisle walls and the seating it provides. The Nave was built to be free and open for assemblies and processions and for Holy Communion daily at the Jesus Altar in front of the stone screen. Above the aisle vaults are covered spaces in what is called the triforium. In some pilgrimage churches these areas were used to accommodate (even overnight) the crowds of pilgrims who visited for the big feasts and festivals.

It is hard for us to imagine what it would have been like. The scale of the Nave dwarfed every other building in Durham including the Castle, and it still does. As it rose above the humble dwellings of the citizens of Durham, the Cathedral was indeed a visible expression of God, a vision made all the more extraordinary by its commanding position on the rock above the river. Not only would the size and magnificence have made an impression on them, but so too would its controlled and wonderful sense of order. Look up and look around! The architectural discipline of the building

Wall Arcading

– the way the spaces are managed and articulated and drawn by the columns, arches, roll mouldings and capitals – is the work of a creative genius. It seemed to reflect the creative genius of God himself. God was the first Creator. Out of chaos he made order and kept it. The Cathedral reflects the order of the creation, the cosmos. Inside it we are invited to find our own place within the creation, and our peace.

Now as then, life can seem brutal, dark, barbarous and cruel. Many people live fractured, broken, disordered lives. It is often hard for us to find purpose or meaning in what happens. God seems hidden or absent. But this wonderful Nave, in its beauty and order, can help to bring God close again. The Cathedral is still the largest building in Durham. It stands as a sign of God's love for us and all creation, a love which nothing can destroy or take away from us.

In front of the Jesus altar at the head of the Nave stood the tombs of the Nevilles, the Lords of Raby. Secular power is never far from people's minds, even in the Church, which has often been too powerful itself. The tombs were subsequently moved at the Reformation to their present position in the south aisle, where they were mutilated. The forces of good and evil, in the Church and in the world and within people's hearts and minds, are usually held in tension. The south side of the Cathedral, the side for the sun, was the side of the angels. The north side, the side away from the sun, was the side of the demons. So as pilgrims moving eastwards through the Nave towards the Crossing, we remember the struggles that abound in and around us as we seek to follow Christ, who is the Way, the Truth and the Life.

18

Our help is in the name of the Lord
who has made heaven and earth.

Loving God, from birth to death you hold us in your
    hand:
make us strong to bear each other's burdens
and humble to share our own,
that as one family we may rest in your power
and trust in your love. Amen.[5]

Looking towards the Central Tower and North Transept

6

The Crossing

When pilgrims arrive at the Crossing they are standing underneath the lantern of the central tower. It is the place to recollect the cross of Christ and his death for us, which is the source of life and hope for us. As pilgrims we cannot understand the fullness of our faith and all its promise without the recognition of Christ's cross at the heart of it.

The Crossing has not always been the centre of the Cathedral in quite this way. In the Middle Ages it was called 'the Great Alley' or 'the Great Aisle'. To the west and the east were the two stone screens covered with their painted sculpture. The screen to the west separated the alley from the people's Nave. The screen to the east separated the alley from the monks' Quire. To north and south the Alley had chapels: in the north transept there were the chapels of St Benedict and St Gregory, and in the south transept there was the chapel of Our Lady of Bolton. The Great Alley was a place of passage, not a place to linger. The clock still stands at its southern end!

The original lantern above our heads was built for a much smaller lower tower topped by a pyramid. The present Crossing arches are over sixty-eight feet in height and are Norman. Everything above the parapet above them dates from the fifteenth century. Perhaps the monks wanted to compete with bigger towers further south! Lightning damage provided the opportunity to rebuild. The final stage of the tower, which you can only see from outside, was built between 1483 and 1490. This final stage now contains the bells which were brought across from the south-west tower. The central tower is 218 feet high. The sculptured detail is still good, even though it is beyond the sight of the unaided human eye

Binoculars are more useful in cathedrals than cameras!

At ground level the furniture around us is Victorian. The work of restoration continued from the time of John Cosin into the eighteenth century and reached its climax in the Victorian restorations of the 1850s and 1870s. Although much was lost in the work of restoration, much was also gained. The Quire was opened up and a new mosaic floor was laid. The original seventeenth-century black-and-white marble pavement was moved to the Crossing. The lectern and the pulpit (for the preaching and interpretation of the Scriptures) were made at the same time. So was Gilbert Scott's screen with its Frosterley marble columns. The Victorians also provided the pews. Their energy and investment saved many of our churches and cathedrals from ruin and decay. In this century at Durham we have been able to improve on the heating and lighting which they installed. Our new architectural lighting has won awards. A modern sound-enhancement system has made it easier to hear throughout the Cathedral. What will the next century give us?

If you look closely at the lectern you will see that the stand which supports the Bible is supported itself by a carving in brass of a pelican. This was a medieval symbol. It was believed that the pelican fed her offspring in the nest with blood from her breast. This symbol, whatever its basis in fact, still reminds us that Christ feeds us, his offspring, through Baptism, with the nourishment of his life and love, declared to us in the Scriptures and the Sacraments.

If you look closely at the pulpit you will see that the stand which supports the book-rest is supported itself by a marble eagle with outstretched wings. This is symbolic of the gospel of Christ being carried around the world. At the foot of the pulpit the columns are supported on the backs of lions. Lions, being royal animals, have always been associated with Christ. In medieval times people believed that lion cubs were born dead (in fact they are born blind) and that after three days they awoke to life; this reminded them of the resurrection of Christ from the dead on the third day at Easter.

So in various ways the Crossing reminds the pilgrim of what Christ has done for us. The life and death and resurrection of Christ are the foundation of the Church's and the Christian's faith – they are its centre, its beginning and its end. As we listen to the gospel message in Scripture we are led to recognize its truth for us and all creation. Christ's love, made clear by and through his cross, is for us the word of life. For the pilgrim it means that in order to experience Christ's life, we must in some measure know his cross.

We adore you, O Christ, and we bless you,
because by your holy cross you have redeemed the world.

Most merciful God,
who by the death and resurrection of your Son Jesus Christ
delivered and saved the world:
grant that by faith in him who suffered on the cross,
we may triumph in the power of his victory,
through Jesus Christ our Lord. Amen.[6]

In the Quire looking towards the Bishop's Throne

7

The Quire

In *The Book of Common Prayer*, to which John Cosin was an important contributor in 1662, there is a famous rubric: 'In Quires and Places where they sing here followeth the Anthem.' The Quire of Durham Cathedral, into which the pilgrim enters through the Gilbert Scott screen, is such a place. Since the sixteenth century the Anglican tradition of church music (offered in the daily offices of Matins and Evensong, which combine the seven daily services of the monks) has developed here and has been passed on through generations of faithful worshippers. Special music continues to be written for the Cathedral, most recently in 1993, so the tradition is strongly maintained.

The Quire is the name given to the part of the Cathedral which accommodates the Dean and Chapter in their daily prayer, and also the choir and the congregation that support them. At present there are a Dean, five Canons, twenty choristers, six choral scholars and six lay clerks. They sing at Evensong on weekdays and at all the Sunday services. Their places are in the choir stalls.

The medieval stalls were probably destroyed by the Scots prisoners of war in 1650. The back rows and the canopies date from Cosin's time. Like the cover or canopy over the Font at the west end, they are strikingly handsome. The front kneeling desks are Victorian additions. Some of the original medieval woodwork may still exist amongst the canopies, but the mend is so invisible that it is hard to tell. The craftsmanship is of a high quality.

Above the canopies on either side are the two sets of pipes for the organ. In the Middle Ages there were four or five organs in the Cathedral. Now there is only one. This is one of the finest organs in the country. At its heart is a seven-teenth-century instrument which has been enlarged over the years by the Durham firm of organ builders, Harrison and Harrison, who still maintain it.

On the north side of the Quire to the east of the stalls is a seventeenth-century pulpit known as Cosin's pulpit. On the south side to the east of the stalls is Bishop Hatfield's Chantry. Hatfield founded Durham House in Oxford, a house specially provided for the Durham monks for study at Oxford's new university. Durham House eventually became Trinity College. Before he died in 1381, Hatfield commis-sioned his own chantry chapel and tomb, and incorporated into the design an episcopal throne for his successors. Here a new Bishop of Durham is 'enthroned' at his service of installation.

In those English cathedrals which were also monastic churches the bishop of the diocese was also the abbot of the monastic community. That was the case here in Durham. As the Bishop/Abbot was away for much of the time, the day-to-day running of the monastery was in the hands of the Prior. Both the Bishop, as Abbot, and the Prior had stalls amongst the monks. In the Middle Ages the monastic community met in the Quire seven times every twenty-four hours to say the seven offices of the day. Offices were a regular time of ordered prayer accompanied by the recita-tion of the Psalms and the reading of Scripture. The first office of the day was Prime, at two o'clock in the morning. The monks processed down into the church from their dormitory and then back again.

'Lord, teach us to pray,' the disciples asked Jesus. The Dean and Chapter still maintain a tradition of daily prayer and praise in this place, and everyone is invited to join them. It is good for pilgrims in the Quire to consider how ordered their own times of prayer may be. We thank God for those who have taught us to pray; for the ceaseless round of prayer which is maintained and offered in sanctuaries like this one; and for the resources – particularly the beautiful gift of music – which enrich prayer and worship.

Let us worship the Lord in the beauty of holiness;
All praise to his name.

Heavenly Father, Creator Spirit,
who in the making of music
has given us a delight for the mind and a solace for
    the heart;
by the harmonies of your grace
resolve the discord of our lives
so that we may sound forth your praise
in what we do and in what we are;
to the glory of your great and wonderful name,
through Jesus Christ our Lord. Amen.[7]

The main altar and Neville Screen

8

The Sanctuary

As we now enter the Quire through the marble Victorian screen designed by Gilbert Scott, above our heads in the first bay where the ribs meet is a carved boss showing the souls of the righteous with the Old Testament patriarch Abraham. This is a reference to the parable told by Jesus in Luke chapter 16 about a rich man named Dives and a beggar named Lazarus. At the end of his life of plenty Dives dies and finds himself in torment, looking across the great divide towards Lazarus, who has also died but is now with Abraham in a place of plenty. This was a popular way of representing paradise, the goal of every faithful Christian. As they processed into their stalls in the Quire for worship, the monks would have believed that their worship would unite them with God, in a sense bringing paradise down to earth. This reminds us that worship brings us to the gate of heaven.

Further on there is a second carved boss in the vault. This one shows the Lamb of God, Christ himself. The Lamb carries a cross over his shoulder – it is a banner or trophy of victory, because on the cross Christ conquered sin and death, and by his resurrection opened the kingdom of heaven to all believers. Like the Passover lamb, Christ offered himself for us as a sacrifice for sin, and God raised him from the dead. This carved boss of the Lamb of God, the Christ, was placed more or less above where the daily Mass or Holy Communion was celebrated by and for the community. Sharing together the sacrament – the heavenly banquet – the monks knew that with God they were in heaven. This is true too for us as we kneel here to receive Communion.

We do not know what the main altar looked like. The

building of the east end of the Cathedral was begun in 1093. In 1104 the shrine of St Cuthbert was placed in the apse of the east end. This shrine was visible behind the main altar. The wooden outer coffin with its painted cover was placed on top of a stone base. In the thirteenth century the shrine was almost hidden from view by a wooden screen. In the fourteenth century this was replaced by the Neville Screen, a gift from the Lords of Raby. It is made of stone from Caen in Normandy. The carving was done in London and was then put together on site. The work is wonderfully delicate. Until the Reformation the niches were filled with 107 painted alabaster statues portraying 'the whole company of heaven'. Mary and the child Jesus were at the centre, with St Cuthbert and St Oswald on either side, and with the Saints of the Church in ranks surrounding them. At the same time Bishop Hatfield was constructing his chantry chapel and episcopal throne in the Quire.

After the damage of the sixteenth and seventeenth centuries, Cosin tidied everything up once again and restored the sanctuary to its former beautiful state. This work continues. The Dean and Chapter restored and cleaned the vault in time for the nine hundredth anniversary of the laying of the foundation stone in 993.

The vault itself replaced the original one which became unsafe after 1235. This was a factor that contributed to the rebuilding of the east end of the Cathedral with a new transept, the Chapel of the Nine Altars. On and around the vault is a wealth of carving. This reflects a later and more decorative style.

Pause now to recollect that this is a holy place built to the glory of God and of all his Saints, especially St Cuthbert. The builders, following an early Christian tradition, patterned the columns with spirals. In this way they marked the place of an altar or the sanctuary of a saint.

The pilgrim stands before the main altar and gives thanks to God for his love revealed in the death and resurrection of Christ, which the sacrament of Holy Communion offers to us, today and for ever. For over 900 years this altar – adorned and loved and beautified – has been the focus of worship and praise in this place, and we pray that it will always be so. The pilgrim prays that God's grace will pour into his own heart and mind as he shares with all God's Church, visible and invisible, the vision of paradise here on earth.

O taste and see how gracious the Lord is.
Happy are they that trust him.

God our Father, you have invited us to share in the supper
which your Son gave to his Church
to proclaim his death until he comes.
May he nourish us by his presence, and unite us in his love;
who is alive and reigns with you and the Holy Spirit,
one God now and for ever. Amen.[8]

The Tomb of Saint Cuthbert

The Shrine of St Cuthbert in the Feretory

The climax of any pilgrim's visit to Durham is seeing the Shrine of St Cuthbert. Move through the doors of the screens to the north or south of the sanctuary, turn east, and then, after descending some steps, you will find the steps that lead to what is called the Feretory.

Here the pilgrims came to pray to God in the presence of the Saint. In medieval times the relics of the Saint inside the coffin were looked upon as a tangible link with paradise. Cuthbert was in heaven but his relics were here on earth. The material relics were the sign of the heavenly reality. Here was a place where heaven and earth met. In the Middle Ages pilgrims came to Cuthbert from all over England and northern Europe. Now they come from all over the world. In this holy place, made holy by Cuthbert and by the prayers of generations, prayer is offered every day by those who want the Saint as their friend.

It is hard for us to know what Cuthbert was really like. All we know is what we are told in Bede's *Life of Cuthbert*. Bede portrays for us a humble, kindly man who befriended the poor and had no fear of authority. In those days people – even kings – went in awe of 'holy men'. Cuthbert also seems to have had a sense of the wonder and goodness of creation. He loved

St Cuthbert's Cross

being alone with the sea, the winds, the hills and the animals. He seems genuinely to have loved people for themselves and showed that God loved them too.

He was born near Melrose around 634. His parents were Christians. As a boy he learned to be a shepherd. Influenced by St Aidan, the first apostle to Northumbria, Cuthbert became a monk. Eventually he became the Abbot of the community that Aidan had founded on Lindisfarne. Then Cuthbert's king asked him to be the bishop of his people. He was their bishop for only two years, since he died on the Outer Farne in 687. At once his monks honoured him and his relics. When the Norsemen invaded the region in the late eighth century, Cuthbert's community took his remains away from Lindisfarne, along with the Lindisfarne Gospels and other precious things. In 995 they made a permanent home for the relics in Durham. A small church was built, and then another replaced it. In 1093 the Normans, the new rulers of a new England, began the third church, the one we see around us today.

The Normans were probably eager to build a great church for Cuthbert because they thought it would be an advantage to befriend him. The North-East was far from settled in those times, and Scotland was not far away.

Before the Normans came to Durham the kings of Wessex had come to honour Cuthbert, bearing gifts. The cult of St Cuthbert spread around the country and in some measure helped to unite it. Pilgrims came in large numbers. A watching loft was erected in the Feretory to supervise them. How they actually came in we do not know; possibly they entered through a door in the outer north Quire aisle. By the thirteenth century more space was needed, and the new Chapel of the Nine Altars was built to accommodate the pilgrims.

Towards the end of the Middle Ages the cult of St

Cuthbert waned. After the surrender of the monastery in 1539 the Shrine was stripped of its wealth and the stonework and metalwork were destroyed. Pilgrimages were forbidden. The Saint's coffin was buried underneath the site of the Shrine. The slabs of Purbeck marble which mark the surround are all that remain of the famous Shrine itself.

Northumbria's most famous king was Oswald. It was he who invited Aidan to Northumbria in the first place. Oswald was a Christian king, and he died fighting the pagan Mercians in 642 near Oswestry on the Welsh borders. Eventually his skull was brought to Lindisfarne, and it was placed with Cuthbert in his coffin. It is still there.

When we stood in front of the main altar we recollected all the Saints of Christendom. Here in the Feretory we recollect the local Saint, our Saint, the Saint who in a special way belongs to the North-East and so to the world.

Your faithful servants bless you, O Lord,
They make known the glory of your Kingdom.

Gracious Lord, we thank you for your servant Cuthbert,
in life a minister of your grace,
in death a channel for your glory.
Grant that in the glad company of your saints
we may journey in faith,
and at the last be brought home
to your dwelling place in joy,
through our Lord and Saviour, Jesus Christ. Amen.[9]

Lindisfarne

10

The Chapel of the Nine Altars

After this I looked, and there before my eyes was a
door opened in heaven, and the voice that I had heard
speaking said, 'Come up here, and I will show you
what must happen hereafter.'

(Revelation 4:1)

As you stand in the Feretory look at the pavement at your
feet, and you will see marked there the line of the original
Norman apse. Underneath will be the foundation stones laid
in 1093. Then look through the wooden Feretory screens.
Look up and look around!

You are looking into the wonderful space of the eastern
transept, which we call the Chapel of the Nine Altars. When
it was decided to enlarge the Cathedral by adding the
transept, the ground level was lowered so as to allow the
clusters of pillars in the new Gothic style to soar to their
great height, giving an extraordinary sense of lightness,
together with the much larger windows that the new style
made possible. Altogether the new east end provided a spa-
cious and dignified area for pilgrims to the shrine and for
altars at which Holy Communion could be celebrated.

It took most of the middle years of the thirteenth century
to complete the Chapel of the Nine Altars and to dedicate the
altars. Architects may have come from Salisbury and sculp-
tors may have come from Lincoln, but the feel of the
transept, dominated by the row of lancet windows on the
east wall, is definitely Northern. The cluster of black marble
columns, rich with fossils, are made from Frosterley marble
quarried in Weardale. The rest of the building stone, like that
throughout the Cathedral, comes from quarries close at

hand. Notice the fine geometrical tracery of the north window facing the public approach to the Cathedral. In contrast, the window on the south side (the private, domestic side) is much plainer.

The nine altars have all gone. They were needed in the thirteenth century because more of the monks, most of whom were laymen, wanted to be ordained as priests. More altars were provided for them to say their daily masses. Now a simple altar furnishes the chapel. Its frontal is a piece of modern embroidery worked by the Cathedral Broderers and given in 1995. It celebrates the coming of Christianity to the North-East, depicting this as a movement from darkness to light. Because we associate this conversion with the Northern Saints, they too are celebrated in the panels behind the altar – from left to right, Cuthbert, Aidan and Bede. Because they were all united in their love of Holy Island or Lindisfarne, the frontal is also a celebration of the natural life and beauty to be found there. In the past Durham Cathedral was full of colour and symbolism. In our own day those who work with the arts and with the crafts can add to its splendour.

The transept is dominated by the rose window. The rose was remodelled in the late eighteenth century. Because the large stone screens have gone, the rose is now the visual climax of the whole Cathedral seen from west to east. When the autumn sun rises behind the rose window it sets the church on fire.

Durham Cathedral is not visited for its medieval glass. It is a great church, however, for the disciples of Clayton and Bell, the Victorian firm that produced stained glass of the highest quality. All the large windows in Durham are filled with their designs and colours. Clayton and Bell deliberately tried to imitate the style, imagery and texture of thirteenth-century glass, and so the scenes in the windows have remained the same as those which were there before. The rose window above the lancets dates from 1877.

> There in heaven stood a throne, and on the throne sat one whose appearance was like the gleam of jasper and cornelian, and round the circle about this throne were twenty-four other thrones, and on them sat twenty-four elders, robed in white and wearing crowns of gold. Each of the elders had a harp, and they held golden bowls of incense, the prayers of God's people, and they were singing a new song: 'Praise and honour, glory and might, to him who sits on the throne and to the Lamb for ever and ever.' And the four living creatures said 'Amen', and the elders fell down and worshipped.
>
> (Revelation 4)

So the visual climax of the Cathedral is the vision of heaven. As pilgrims we are drawn in through the mystery of our faith through the mystery of Christ towards the worship of heaven. We join the four and twenty elders and their attendant cherubim and seraphim in the worship of God our Father, who is the Beginning and the End of all that was, all that is and all that will be.

In the first circle of the rose window you can see the twelve apostles. Look above to the circular well boss at the centre of the chapel vault, and you will see, carved in stone, the four apostles with their attendant symbols – the lion and St Mark, the ox and St Luke, the human and St Matthew and the eagle and St John. Behind you in the Feretory is St Cuthbert. You are surrounded by the prayers of the Saints and the prayers of the Church. The rose is also the symbol of Mary. She too has accompanied us from the first moment of Annunciation in the Galilee. With her for inspiration, guidance and example, we too may be found by God: and to her, as the Patron of this Cathedral church, we pray that we too may respond to his call.

When they built the Chapel of the Nine Altars the monks of Durham were not simply building a Gothic *tour de force*. They were bringing the whole Cathedral to its completion. They were making it possible for Christian pilgrims like us to find their faith and to celebrate it in all its fullness.

> With this in mind, then, I kneel in prayer to the Father from whom every family in heaven and on earth takes its name, that out of the treasures of his glory he may grant you strength and power through his Spirit in your inner being, that through faith Christ may dwell in your hearts in love. With deep roots and firm foundations, may you be strong to grasp, with all God's people, what is the breadth and length and height and depth of the love of Christ, and to know it, though it is beyond knowledge. So may you attain to fullness of being, the fullness of God himself.
>
> (Ephesians 3:14–19)

Great is the Lord and greatly to be praised.
There is no end to his greatness.

One generation shall praise your works to another
And shall declare your power.

All your works praise you, O Lord,
And your faithful servants bless you.

They make known the glory of your Kingdom
And speak of your power.

My mouth shall speak the praise of the Lord.
Let all flesh bless his holy name for ever.

Merciful God,
you have prepared for those who love you
such good things as pass our understanding.
Pour into our hears such love towards you
that we, loving you above all things,
may obtain your promises,
which exceed all that we can desire,
through Jesus Christ our Lord. Amen.[10]

11

'Go in Peace to Love and Serve the Lord'

A pilgrimage is more than an exercise in spiritual self-indulgence! We seek God and try to open ourselves up to him, so that he may find us and make us more like himself. It is time now to leave the vision of heaven and to make the world more like the heaven that we have glimpsed.

As the pilgrim leaves the Cathedral there are a number of different features to remind us of the need to obey Christ's call to follow him. We follow him in the particular place in which we live, in the nation of which we are a part, and in the world to which we all belong.

Take the south Quire aisle out of the Chapel of the Nine Altars. On the right as you pass the bottom of the Feretory steps you will see the names of the Bishops, Priors and Deans of Durham since 995, when Aldhun was the first Bishop. In many different ways these men have served God in and around this place.

Further along the aisle on the south you will see our latest window. It was given in 1997 to celebrate the millennium of Durham diocese in 1995. A thousand years have passed since the time when Cuthbert's coffin arrived here and Aldhun became the first Bishop. The top part of the window celebrates the importance of Cuthbert in the events before 995. The bottom part celebrates some of the things that have dominated or influenced people's lives in this area for a thousand years.

The picture of glass blowing, for example, reminds us of an industry that has been important to the Sunderland area since the time of Bede. Ship-building and coal mining have been vital to the region's economy since the Middle Ages. The Stockton and Darlington Railway brought coal to the

Tees, and Stockton became a centre for steel making. Electricity is now generated by the power station at Hartlepool. Old industries have gone, new ones have come, and people's lives have been changed. Motor cars and computers are now made in County Durham. Another new industry is leisure and recreation. Only the agricultural industry has remained constant over a thousand years. Sheep farming is still essential for the livelihood of the dales.

At the bottom of the window a bishop and a miner are portrayed as about to shake hands. In the nineteenth century a Bishop of Durham involved himself in an industrial dispute and helped to make peace. The Church's social role is one of reconciliation, of seeking justice and peace. The millennium window reminds us that we must serve the place and neighbourhood in which we live.

Almighty Father,
whose Son Jesus Christ has taught us
that what we do for the least of our brothers and
 sisters
we do also for him;
give us the will to be the servant of others
as he was the servant of all,
who gave up his life and died for us,
but is alive and reigns with you and the Holy Spirit,
one God, now and for ever. Amen.[11]

12

The Nation

As you walk back down the south aisle, reflect that the industries portrayed in the millennium window are of more than local or even regional interest. Approaching the south transept, you will be reminded again of the mining industry. High up on the wall facing you is the Haswell Lodge banner, one of the oldest lodge banners. Further along the aisle towards the west of the Nave is the Miner's Memorial. Many, many lives were lost in accidents and disasters in the pits. Our landscape is full of memories. Every year on Gala Day ex-miners and their families return to the Cathedral to remember their dead. The mining industry changed and shaped the lives of millions, not just in County Durham but throughout the nation.

As you turn into the south transept on the left you will notice the chapel set aside for the Durham Light Infantry. The regiment no longer exists but has been amalgamated into the Infantry Regiment. The chapel commemorates all those who served in the DLI. It celebrates a long and distinguished military history. It commemorates those who have died in war defending our nation's life and liberty. The books record the known names of those who fell. People come from all over the world to refer to them. Above are some of the battle honours and standards which have been laid up.

Christians hope that never again will we see wars such as those which have blighted this century. However, wars are still being fought, and they affect us all in different ways. But we are called to serve in other ways: to promote justice in our land as well as peace, to support the weak as much as the strong, and to strive and even to suffer for what is good.

Christ invites us to be the servants of others, just as he was the willing servant of all.

On the opposite side of the south transept and under the miners' banner is the finest nineteenth-century monument in the Cathedral. It is in memory of Shute Barrington, who was Bishop of Durham from 1791 to 1826. This was the time of the French Revolution and the Napoleonic Wars. In this country the people were then crying out for reform in every area of the nation's life.

Bishop Barrington lived in stirring times. But he was also involved in the life of literature and art. He was a friend of Sir Walter Scott, and through him he would have known about the poets and painters of the Romantic Movement. This is a good place for the Christian pilgrim to recollect the important part which the arts play in our lives. Durham features in Scott's poetry, and also in Turner's paintings. It continues to be an inspiration. Some of our stained-glass windows, like the millennium window, are works of modern art. The 'daily bread' window by the north door and the windows in the Galilee commemorating Bede and Mary are good examples. The Cathedral is always pleased to make links with modern art. This too is part of the national heritage of this extraordinary church.

✠

God of righteousness and truth,
grant to our Sovereign and our government,
and to all in positions of influence and responsibility,
the guidance of your Holy Spirit.
May they never lead the nation wrongly
but always love righteousness and truth.
So may your kingdom come
and your name be hallowed;
through Jesus Christ our Lord. Amen.[12]

13

The World

If you cross to the north side of the Great Alley into the north transept you will find to your right the Gregory Chapel. The Reserved Sacrament is there, so the chapel is set aside as a place of prayer.

The Gregory who is commemorated there was the Pope who in 597 sent Augustine to Canterbury to convert the English. Gregory's prayer resulted in action! He also sent Paulinus. Augustine sent Paulinus to York. It was Paulinus who baptized Edwyn at York. Edwyn was the first Northumbrian king to become a Christian. So the links between the North-East and Europe are strong.

The altar which stands against the north wall of the transept is dedicated to St Benedict, the founder of Western monasticism. Gregory was a monk and he was so impressed by Benedict's influence that he wrote a book about the life of St Benedict. Benedict gave his monks a Rule, by which they ordered their individual and community life. The Benedictine communities of monks and nuns still live by his Rule today.

In 597 England would have seemed a strange and foreign place to Augustine and Paulinus. By all accounts, they turned back at least once before they finally arrived. The Romans had left Britain almost two centuries before, so to the two monks it would have seemed to be an inhospitable and unfriendly land, an offshore island separated from civilization and progress. That is exactly how some English people today think of other places in the world that are foreign to them.

As strange and foreign, for instance, as Africa? On the wall to the left of the Benedict altar hangs the Lesotho banner.

Since 1986 the diocese of Durham has been linked with the diocese of Lesotho. Lesotho itself is an independent sovereign state, though it is surrounded completely by the Republic of South Africa. The banner is made of mohair and it was designed and woven by the Basotho. It illustrates some of the projects which the inter-diocesan link has supported. A banner was also made and designed here, and this now hangs in the cathedral in Maseru, Lesotho's capital.

This link symbolizes our connections with the world and its concerns. Many people come to Durham from all over the world – people from different Christian traditions, people of other faiths, people of no faith at all. Because God is the Creator of all that is, and because his Church is universal, our Christian concerns cannot be limited to our homes or our nation. We are citizens of the world, and with Christ we seek justice, peace and dignity for the entire human race.

God bless Africa
guard her children
guide her leaders
and give her peace;
for Jesus Christ's sake. Amen.[13]

Almighty God,
from whom all thoughts of truth and peace proceed:
kindle, we pray, in the hearts of everyone
the true love of peace;
and guide with your pure and peaceable wisdom
those who take counsel for the nations of the world;
that in tranquillity your kingdom may go forward,
till the earth is filled with the knowledge of your love;
through Jesus Christ our Lord. Amen.[14]

14

And Finally…

Look south across the Great Alley. The far wall of the south transept is dominated by Prior Castell's clock. Time passes. It is time to move on.

This famous clock was installed between 1496 and 1519. What a difference it must have made to the ordering of the monastery's life in those final days. It is a fine instrument. Restored in 1938, it still keeps time. It has kept time through many changes, and multitudes of people have read its hands, as we do. It is time to go.

Before you leave the Cathedral you may wish to light a candle at one of the votive candle stands in the Nave. This may be to say thank you to God for your pilgrimage; or you may wish to pray for someone you love or someone you know who is in need. It may be a prayer for the world, which is always in need of justice, peace and healing. You may wish to write down your prayer so that it may be offered the following morning at the daily Eucharist.

Please remember that the Cathedral and those who care for it also need your prayers. It is a marvellous building, a work of human ingenuity and achievement. Yet to some it speaks of power. Power is abused when pride takes the place of reverence, awe and wonder. In our freedom we often get things badly wrong. It is possible for God's glory and loving care for his creation to be distorted by our ambitions.

The story of this Cathedral casts its shadow. Please pray that those who care for it and those who use it daily may seek only the good of all God's people, in spirit and in truth.

✠

Yours, Lord, is the greatness, the power,
the glory, the splendour, and the majesty;
for everything in heaven and on earth is yours.
All things come from you,
and of your own do we give you.

(1 Chronicles 29:11–12)

The north door will take you back to Palace Green, to the University and the City. The south-west door will take you to the Cloisters, the College and the riverbanks. Which ever way you go, you will be returning to the business of the world – to shops and restaurants and libraries and offices and gardens and homes, on foot, by car or by rail.

The West Towers

✠

Almighty God,
in Christ you have made all things new:
transform the poverty of our nature
by the riches of your grace,
and in the renewal of our lives
make known your heavenly glory. Amen.[15]

Go in peace, with God to enfold you,
God in your speaking, God in your thinking,
God in your sleeping, God in your waking,
God in your watching, God in your hoping,
God in your life, God on your lips,
God in your hearts, and in your eternity. Amen.[16]

Coming and Going

Standing here in the quiet nave
Coming in out of the busy world
Suddenly moved to push the heavy door
Into the sanctuary,
I wait now in the dimness,
Unsure of where to look or how to see,
Getting my bearings,
Knowing I should do this and this –
But, for myself, uncertain.

Sitting now in a side chapel
Feeling a growing sense of awe
Ready to look beyond my hesitation
Up to the roof beam,
I catch my breath in wonder
At stone upon stone climbing to far off heaven,
Suddenly overwhelmed,
Knowing that ordinary folk
Could aim so high and certain.

Kneeling at length upon the worn stone
Wanting to feel myself in touch
Suddenly glad of symmetry and light
In far perspective,
I seek my own direction
Moved by a faith that dared to build in stone,
Getting my bearings,
Knowing I might do this and this –
Now, for myself, more certain.

Anne Castling[17]

References

1. *Alternative Service Book*, p. 324, © The Central Board of Finance of the Church of England.
2. Ibid., p. 763.
3. Ibid., p. 237.
4. Ibid., p. 127.
5. The Society of St Francis
6. *Alternative Service Book*, p. 522, op. cit.
7. Peter Baelz, Durham Cathedral
8. *Lent, Holy Week and Easter*, p. 183, Church House Publishing.
9. Durham Cathedral.
10. *Alternative Service Book*, p. 745, op. cit.
11. *Alternative Service Book*, p. 552.
12. *Celebrating Common Prayer*, p. 248.
13. Bishop Huddleston's Prayer for Africa, Oxford Book of Prayer, no 206, Oxford University Press.
14. *Alternative Service Book*, p. 912, op. cit.
15. Ibid., p. 476.
16. A Celtic prayer.
17. Coming and Going, Anne Castling, *The Spirit of the Cathedral*.